Fire and Entrepren<br>
preser

# The Cookboo
# For Your Probationary
# Firefighters & First
# Responders

Become a Great Cook and an
Even Greater Firefighter or First
Responder
By Michael W.L. Fields
Copyright © 2020

☐

Printed in the United States of America

First Printing, 2020

Fire and Entrepreneurship Services publishing

fire-and-entrepreneurship-services.com

☐

# Contents

# Introduction: Who I Am

Hi, I am Michael Fields. I have been a Firefighter for over ten years, four years active duty Army, and going on six years of civil service as a firefighter as of 2020. Since 2010 when I first joined the fire service, I have created great relationships not only in the fire service but through multi agencies during calls, major incidents, educational classes, and training. And I have learned that most agencies have the same probationary rules and responsibilities.

I wanted to write a book that is not only a guide to becoming a probationary firefighter or first responder, but also a cookbook to share my passion for cooking that I have found while working in the fire service. I originally wanted to make this book only for the fire service, but I honestly think any agency would benefit from this book or anyone who just wants to know how to start to learn the basics of cooking.

Sit back and enjoy it! I hope that you are as lucky as I am with getting to become part of the brother and sisterhood of first responders and have the opportunity to create great relationships, lifelong friendships, and become part of a family together.

☐

# Chapter 1:  Don't Forget Where You Come From

As a new firefighter/first responder, you will most likely become the station cook, until a new employee comes on to the floor on your shift as the new probie. (Probie: is a term used by firefighters to identify a probationary firefighter, or rookie.)  When I started out in civil service as a firefighter, I was the new guy for two years. I had no clue how to cook except when I had to call my mom and ask for recipes (which was also very embarrassing as a 21-year-old). I had to quickly learn how to become a cook for 5 to 7 people every night that I was working. We worked 48 hours on and 72 hours off, so you can probably imagine how much time I had to really experiment with cooking and creating meals, not only for dinner but somedays breakfast was expected. Because of the structure fires, car fires, medicals, car accidents, wildland fires, vehicle rollovers, and other incidents, I hardly had time to plan a meal.  I had to quickly learn how to prepare meals that I could throw together within just 20 minutes at times. I was not perfect. I don't think I actually received a legit compliment until almost the first anniversary of my cooking duties. I think it was my homemade biscuits and gravy recipe that I made that impressed our chief on duty and a lot of others I worked with every day.  Beyond that point, the compliments started rolling in almost every meal!

I endured many trials and tribulations not only while working as a firefighter but also as a cook for the fire station. If you are a new first responder coming into this job, I implore you to have an open mind. When the older, seasoned people you work with were young, they did have it a lot worse. So, please don't look at this as a form of hazing. Instead, look at this as a rite of passage to becoming a trusted brother in the brotherhood of firefighters and first responders. You may think that this is unfair, but I promise you those guys you work with do not care about your feelings. They are going to make sure you are committed, trustworthy, and willing to do the job. They want to have confidence in you to pull them out of a burning building when the time comes!

During this time, you need to grow a thick skin and not take every comment personally. Instead, sit back and listen to feedback or instructions. Take the advice and do what you can to correct what you may have done wrong. The problem with our generation and others to come into the first responder services is everyone takes offense to any negative comments made by other firefighters or first responders. Do not take them personally. Yes, there may be some not so complimentary comments made at times, but most of them are for you not to defend or say anything, but to listen and learn. Next, I am going to include a few of the many important tasks, duties, and responsibilities that you should complete daily. If you follow these tasks alone without question or guidance, you will quickly gain the respect of any seasoned firefighter, first responder, or other people you work with daily. Yes, they may not show it. But in due time, when they see your hard work and dedication, you will eventually see the light and compliments will be given once you are a trusted and respected member of the brotherhood. Remember, you physically live with the members of your team or at least spend half of your life with them. Like it or not, this is your second family, so treat them as so. Their families will also become part of yours down the road. When you get the chance to invite your girlfriend or wife and kids, take that opportunity. That is an invitation for you to introduce your primary family to your secondary family.
☐

# Chapter 2:  Tasks, Duties, and Responsibilities

After I explain the Tasks, Duties, and Responsibilities, I will explain in detail the cookbook side of this book.

Tasks, Duties, and Responsibilities to follow:

1.     Arrive at least 30 minutes before your shift, especially your first shift. Personally, I would arrive one hour early, so you know your route to work, in case you have an emergency, or stop for food or gas for the trip. (I would at least bring food for yourself for your shift including breakfast, lunch, dinner, and snacks).

2.     If you need gear, find out where to get the items you need. If you have it ahead of time, find out your assignment located on a clipboard or paper somewhere either near the chief's office or on the daily meeting table. Also, try and get your gear out near the truck and position you are assigned to before morning shift change. (You are expected to do this yourself every day on shift. Do not wait for someone to tell you where you are at for the day!) If you have questions or cannot find the daily assignments, ask your first officer in charge of you, an LT, or Lead Firefighter, for example.

3.      Coffee and/or tea is expected to be made so on your first day or first few shifts. Pay attention to the coffee pot and make sure it is not empty. If it is empty, ask how much coffee to use and keep a pot of coffee on always—or at least until 5 p.m. each and every day! Wait for someone to tell you when you should not make coffee. Some stations require a pot on eight hours a day. Some even make sweet tea daily.  When I was in the fire service in Texas, Station 1 required three pitchers of sweet tea to be made daily along with coffee in the morning. Sweet tea consisted of 1 pitcher with 3 cups of sugar mixed in, another pitcher with 2 cups of sugar mixed in, and the last pitcher has no sugar. The tea used was any great local black tea, but if you don't know, then ask.  And, just as a side note, if you serve as a first responder in the south, your chief will have a coffee cup or tea glass they do not wash. (DO NOT WASH THIS CUP OR GLASS. YOU WILL HEAR ABOUT IT, AND NOT SO NICE WORDS WILL BE SHARED BY THE CHIEF TO YOUR FACE. I don't know from experience personally, but I have heard of a particular person who did this, and the conversation wasn't pleasant)!

4.      If breakfast is expected, make sure you ask what everyone wants to eat for your next shift for breakfast (the next time you work), or you can run to the store to get food and get what they would like to eat. Sometimes a local taco shop is a bit easier, especially on busy days. Some restaurants give discounts to first responders who show up in uniform. Picking up food to go could be cheaper than buying the groceries needed to make breakfast.  In this book, I have a lot of great recipes to choose from for meals.

5.    If you have questions, always ask your LT or Lead Firefighter (for example, your first ranking person). Never go above them unless there is a life-threatening issue or that person is being incompetent in their duties and/or a direct violation of what they should be doing. Never bother the chiefs unless asked to do so or if they call you into their office. If you are called in their office, stand straight with your hands either behind you in parade rest, straight to your sides, or in front of you interlocked. Do not lean anywhere or stand with your hands in your pockets. Always answer with yes sir or their rank, for example (Yes chief, or Captain.

6.    You will most likely be given a probie book, which should include tasks or training you will need to complete and/or finish in a specified time. If a time limit is not given, then create a time frame for yourself and achieve this as soon as possible. Stay on top of these tasks. Sometimes you may need to request others to help with training or a job in your task book, but do not bother your coworkers during lunchtime, workouts, or after hours. Unless you are ordered to do so, these are considered relax times. Be consistent with asking, but do not drive your coworkers crazy with making them train you or making them sign things. Eventually, it will all come together.

7.     Workout times: As a new employee, I always wait to see who on my shift works out. I would personally workout later, depending on the size of your gym at work, or they may have a designated time they go to the gym near the fire station. Always work out and stay in shape both mentally and physically. However, do not crowd your seasoned coworkers, allow them to do their thing, and work around them! I have also worked out with some departments that have a scheduled team workout each day. I would always get in on those workouts when possible! It also may be in your best interest to eventually create team workouts and ask if anybody wants to join. This alone helps your coworkers get to know you a bit better. And yes, not everyone likes to work out, but having that positive energy helps with the way people perceive you. At least you won't be the lazy guy. But, don't use this workout time being the suck-up, teacher's pet, or brown nose by doing these workouts. People use team workouts at times to look good for promotions—don't be this guy either. Remember, the more time you spend with your coworkers, the greater your relationships will be. Be honest and consistent with who you are as a person and a first responder. Remember where you came from and always keep that selfless service and integrity mentality.

8.     It's okay to do college or school at work, but make sure you are doing that on your own free time --you may have free time after hours. It also may be fun to join in on card games and fun activities with your employers, but always remember your duties, tasks, and responsibilities come first! Work will come first over anything else you do in your free time! In my opinion, I would not bring video games, schoolwork, or anything else for at least one month. During this time, you can better understand the flow and not make anybody upset by being distracted.

9.      Always be the first one to do your station chores or at least start them; some departments will have a daily chore list. Some stations will have a designated time in which to do them. Find that schedule and learn each day you work what chore you will be doing. Don't have to be asked to do them!

10.     Training: Every day, at least during the weekdays, you will have training. Most training is held in the afternoon. You will be expected to learn how to create classes from scratch. Learn how to do this as soon as you can, so it will be easier the next time you have to create a class. PowerPoint will be your best friend, but also your station should have educational books that you used in school. Or, you can elect to do more hands-on classes. This provides an excellent opportunity to leave the station and get to know your area better or to mark off tasks in your probie book. Don't be afraid to ask for help if you don't know something.  Know the proper time to ask questions and don't ask a million questions at once. Try to learn on your own before you ask any questions.

11.     If dinner is expected, ask where you can go shopping. You should ask what people like and cook accordingly.  If someone offers to cook, ask to help. Always, if you can, eat with the station crew. Mealtime can be a time for building relationships with your crew. If you cannot eat what they eat, make a side where you can still eat and pay for your share accordingly.  The recipes in this book provide recipes for many meal alternatives.

12.    After dinner, the cook usually does not clean the dishes, but as a new employee, expect to help with cleaning. They may even make you do all dishes and clean, so expect the worst! But always clean even when told you don't have to do so. Cleaning duties may include washing dishes, wiping down counters and dinner table, cleaning out coffee pots (unless the coffee is freshly made), taking out the trash, sweeping and mopping the floors, and loading and starting the dishwasher!

13.    As a new probie, be expected to be that last one awake and the first one to be up. As the last one asleep, you are to make sure the station is locked up, and all chores are completed. You will ensure that the dishes are out of the sink; the dishwasher is started; the coffee is in the pot and ready to start the next morning; and the floors are mopped, swept, and ready for a new day's work.

14.    Be the first one up and awake in the morning! Unlock the station, start the coffee—make two pots if needed! Have plenty of coffee hot and ready! Unload the dishwasher(s). Fold dish towels and truck towels and put them away. Some stations may require you to print out the schedule for the day or post it somewhere. Ask your upline supervisor about it the night before and move your gear accordingly to where you are supposed to be the next day!

15.    Be the first one at the morning meeting table or place of shift change. Always be in proper uniform, clean-shaven, teeth brushed, hair brushed, and showered with deodorant!

16.    Other things you should know that I did not list above are:

- Do not do laundry after 7 p.m.
- Do not work out after 7 p.m. for the first month or whenever it is expected.
- Do not sit in the TV room unless you're at roll call or unless told it's okay.
- Never sit in the chief's chair at the morning meeting table.
- Do not participate in extracurricular activities unless told its okay. Expect to be exiled for a bit during your probationary time, but do not take offense. Work on your mental strength during this time.
- Read everything you can about the fire service, including your local SOP's and SOG's (standard operating procedures and guides) or any books about basic fire service knowledge.
- When you check your vehicle as a driver, make sure you always have fuel and water. If you are on a brush truck or wildland vehicle, make sure pony motor filters are changed daily, MRE's or meals are on the truck, and proper equipment is on the truck. Even if you are not the driver, make sure the hydrant bag has the correct wrenches and tools. Make sure there is fresh water on the vehicles—especially yours.
- Be sure your SCBA or equipment is properly checked and functioning every morning, even on weekends!
- Always keep two pens and a small, waterproof notebook in your pockets.
- Always do what you are told and follow your chain of command in every aspect of your career.

17. Always follow your department's Core Values. I was in the Army for four years as an active duty soldier. Listed below are the seven values that I followed in the military, and I still follow them daily in my normal life inside and outside of work!

a.      Loyalty: Bear true faith and Allegiance to your department and your country. A Loyal first responder is one who supports the leadership and fellow employers. Do your share and show loyalty to your department and brother/sisterhood.

b.      Duty: Fulfill your obligations. Be able to accomplish tasks as part of a team.

c.      Respect:  Treat others with respect. Treat people how you would want to be treated.

d.      Selfless Service: Put the welfare of your country and subordinates before your own. In serving your country, you are doing your duty loyally without thought of recognition or gain.

e.      Honor: Honor is living the values of respect, duty, loyalty, selfless service, integrity, and personal courage in everything you do!

f.      Integrity: Do what is right, legally, and morally.  If you mess up, fess up! Do not hide it!

g.      Personal Courage: Face fear, danger, and adversity (physically and morally).   Endure physical duress, and sometimes you may endure risking personal safety to save the lives of others.  Make peace with your job title. That may be what you have to do to save a life!

h.      The Army Warrior ethos includes:  I will always place the mission first. I will never accept defeat. I will never quit. I will never leave a fallen comrade. (These are also great to live by as a first responder).

All these tasks, duties, and responsibilities are a large part of who you are and who you will become as a first responder. Follow these, and you will not only become a better person mentally, morally, and physically but will also gain respect for and from your coworkers who have been doing what you do for 10 to 20 years! Adhering to these values will also show you who you can trust and not to trust and follow. Follow a firefighter or lead firefighter who supports these values listed above, and always strive to be the best first responder you can possibly be!

□

# Chapter 3: My Journey in the Fire Service Through Cooking

Now I will take you on a journey that I went through to become a cook for the fire service. I implore anybody just learning to cook to follow this guide and take bits and pieces out of it to become a future chef or even just a basic cook that can prepare a meal without using measuring cups and spoons for every recipe. Most recipes serve five to seven people just because that is how I've learned to cook in the fire service. You can easily split the recipes by dividing the recipe in half and make a meal for two or three people. Likewise, you can multiply it by 2 to cook for 10 to 14 people. I also ask that you take the time and cook these recipes multiple times. Challenge yourself each time to either add an ingredient that will go with the dish or try not to use measuring cups or spoons. Doing this helps you create meals in your head that you can make "from scratch." I used to have a pen and paper to write down detailed directions for shopping for groceries and cooking a meal. Now, I can go to the store and mentally pick up everything I need. Then, I can create a dish that I've never cooked based on my knowledge of basic seasonings and experience with cooking different meals. I enjoy watching cooking channels to get new ideas or research online for new creations. After you get your coworkers to open up to you, you may get great ideas and recipes from them about their favorite dishes. They may even help you cook some nights at work.

To get started, I suggest that you ask your crew what meals they would like to eat. Find out if anyone is allergic to any items you cook with and or if anyone does not prefer a specific type of food such as spicy foods. This information gives you a broad but useful idea of what you can cook. You will also know which items to substitute in the different dishes you are going to cook. If you cannot follow this recipe in this cookbook due to substitutions, then search on the Internet to help you with your selections. You might search for "Hamburgers with no (ingredient)." This search should populate recipes without that ingredient or a substitution for that ingredient. Also, think about substitutions, such as if you cannot put jalapenos into something, maybe green peppers would be a good item to add instead. Some dishes listed in this guide may be spicy, but spicy items can be easily substituted. I will list these items that are spicy so you can plan accordingly.

Once you know what your crew likes, it will become easier to know what to cook each night that you work—"Taco Tuesdays" or "Wing Wednesdays." For starters, I advise you to come up with a schedule (weekends and holidays may be more relaxed). You can do bigger meals like pinto bean soup or Green Chili Sloppers on those days. On the days when you cook a larger meal, you have the opportunity to provide a meal to other stations. We used to invite Station 1 and 2 to our Station 5. Because of our proximity, the staff could eat at our station and still respond to their district promptly if called. On the weekdays, try and stick to something easy that can be cook within an hour or so. Obviously, being a new cook, it will take longer at first but try to work it down to a quick meal as time goes.

Next, I would like to talk about the costs of meals and different funds and ideas that help you better organize meal plans for your station. I suggest that management maintain a lockbox to keep track of the money received and taken out. The money should be counted frequently to ensure funds are put in and taken out appropriately. A balance sheet should be kept to document all transactions. This method provides a check and balance on the funds. This method holds everyone accountable for paying their fair share. I like this idea because it keeps everyone responsible at work to pay for whichever meal you buy and make for everyone. Also, this method takes out the factor that someone can blame you for taking more money than what the meal is worth. So, as an example: Everyone at the station pitches 20 bucks for the money box to start. If you have five people, then that's $100. Then, you take what you need to get dinner—let's say you take out $50 and dinner was $47. Everyone pays $10, and the extra money gets put back into the box instead of your pocket. That way down the road, when the box may have extra money, you might be able to buy a steak dinner for everyone based on the extra money paid to the box. To make them accountable, I like to take the total amount owed for dinner or the present meal and write it on a board or piece of paper. The paper shows everyone's name and the cost of the meal per person. When they pay the amount owed, write paid next to their name. This method works great and is very straightforward. It keeps people honest. Others hassle them if they did not pay, which also helps! Just ensure once they pay, you tell the person who oversees the money box. They should place the funds in the box and balance the box if need be. I would be lying if I said you wouldn't lose any money as a new employee cooking for everyone, so if you don't learn anything else in this book, always make sure you get paid or at least try to!

Sometimes it's good to splurge! I used to provide dessert at no cost to them once a week. They enjoyed that, and it helped because they obviously found out I was paying for it myself. When you do this, people sometimes offer to pay for your portion of the dinner. If you have issues with not getting paid, especially from specific individuals, then you can always contact your first line lead firefighter or supervisor. It may be shocking to you, but not everyone is honest or will pay you. Sometimes they just need a little reminding from a boss but only do this if there is a real issue. If you report to the boss all the time and don't give them a chance to pay, you can lose respect and trust from your employees. I usually give them until the next shift to pay me unless it becomes a habit, then I request it that same day!

☐

# Chapter 4: Meal Prepping and Diets

Always pay attention to your coworker's diets. You may work with people who only eat vegan or vegetarian meals. You do not always have to cater to people with specific diets, but once you're comfortable with cooking and they want in on a meal, then research how to substitute meat for meatless vegan. In today's world, we have many more people eating specific diets and meals that are healthier than what we may have learned from older coworkers and family members. In fact, cooking healthier may upset a seasoned coworker or chief, but if their hungry, they will eat—trust me on this! Just make the decision based on the popularity of the station! You can always replace carbs and starches such as pasta and bread with no carbs or gluten-free bread or pasta. Squash noodles or spaghetti squash provide an excellent vegetable option for pasta as well. Meatless vegan options are available nowadays. Meat substitutes are great and look and taste like meat but are meatless! My favorites include prepared frozen chicken strips or nuggets. Many stores also carry a meatless vegan ground beef. These vegan and meatless options are expensive but do taste like the real thing. In this book, I have many great recipes to choose from for meals. Some healthier condiment options include low-sodium and no-sugar items such as soy sauce, sugar-free ranch dressing, or light mayo. Just watch and listen to your coworkers. Then, research your options and make meal choices based on what your shift likes the most.

Meal prepping makes a difference in food costs and can save you a lot of money. For example, green chilis—you can get a bushel from the market, roast them, peel them, and freeze them. Then, all year, you have options to make green chili with anything and everything. Another example is salad. You can purchase prepared salad that you still need to wash at $5 to $8 a container. Or, you purchase two heads of lettuce at less than a quarter of the price, get four times as much lettuce, and prepare the salad yourself. It may be time-consuming, but those small changes make a difference in your meal being $5 with items you prepared yourself or $8 when made from prepared items. Remember, people do not want to eat an $8 meal every time you cook! Your job is not only to cook but stay on a budget. Get online and look at your local grocery stores for deals on food items you can use to prepare your meals. Some grocery stores allow you to get a full meal with everything in the advertisement. You might get some ice cream or a pie for free. Pay attention to grocery store advertisements or even restaurant meals for great ideas!

☐

# Chapter 5: Cook with Spontaneity and Passion

Cook with spontaneity and passion. I, for one, am not an exact measurement kind of guy, but I strive for perfection in this cookbook. I implore you to use multiple spoons to taste test your food while cooking and add or remove ingredients to make these recipes your own or create something amazing yourself! Make new recipes and pass them on to your children, families, or your new probies and first responders.

A few things are great to have at the station or your home for cooking. This list is where I like to start. Eventually, you can get all these items if you so choose! I would also suggest getting one or two items every time you go to the store. Getting everything at one time can be costly.

Some of the items are already prepared for time's sake but get as much fresh stuff as you can to make your dishes taste better.

- ☐ Seasoned salt
- ☐ Italian seasonings (basil, oregano, parsley fresh)
- ☐ Chili powder
- ☐ Cumin
- ☐ Sea salt
- ☐ Cracked black pepper
- ☐ Garlic powder
- ☐ Minced garlic (jar)
- ☐ Minced Ginger (jar)
- ☐ Gourmet Burger Seasoning
- ☐ Olive oil
- ☐ Coconut oil
- ☐ Italian seasoned breadcrumbs
- ☐ Eggs
- ☐ Mayo (Blue Plate)

- ☐ White distilled vinegar
- ☐ Flour
- ☐ Sugar (Honey or agave, for substitutes)
- ☐ Sesame oil
- ☐ Sesame seeds
- ☐ Sushi or rice seasoning
- ☐ Sour cream (Large container)
- ☐ Brown sugar
- ☐ Your favorite BBQ sauces
- ☐ Peanut butter
- ☐ Jelly
- ☐ Bread
- ☐ Saltine crackers
- ☐ Angel hair or thin spaghetti or any pasta
- ☐ Pasta sauce or tomato sauce to make homemade sauce

Everything listed above is great to have in your home pantry or for your station's food kitty fund. My past food kitty funds had all this, and it cost about $14 a month. You may be asked to do a fund such as this. These are some great ideas to help you get started. As a rule, just make sure you are getting paid. Setting up an online payment portal helps because most people do not carry cash anymore.

Today cooking is a lost art. The meals you create yourself will be remembered and valued. Food is not only for sustenance, but also it helps create great memories with family and friends. So, do not cook on my behalf—Cook for yourself. Cook to learn something new. Cook because it is your passion.

This book is not just for first responders; it is for anyone willing to pick up a cooking apron and get to work creating meals from recipes and living life through food, love, laughter, and experiences. I hope you love these recipes just as much as I do.

These recipes are from my family to yours. I wish you all a long prosperous life filled with family and friends and exciting, lifelong experiences. And remember, you can do anything you put your mind to, if only you put the effort in to do so!

# Beef Dishes:

# Anything but Basic Burgers

Ingredients:

- ☐ 3 pounds ground beef - 93/7 preferred
- ☐ 1 to 1 ½ cups BBQ sauce – use your favorite brand
- ☐ 1 tablespoon minced garlic
- ☐ 2 eggs
- ☐ ¼ to ½ cup Italian breadcrumbs

Preferred cooking: Gas, Charcoal, Pellet, or Smoker grill.
Pre-heat your grill to between 375 degrees and 425 degrees

Instructions:

1. Start by placing ground beef in a large mixing bowl, add eggs, and BBQ sauce. This makes a wet consistency. You want it wet, but not soaking the meat. I would add the amount listed at a minimum.

2. Next, add minced garlic, mix thoroughly.

3. Then add Italian breadcrumbs slowly, mixing it in till you have a consistency where the meat holds together very well, but do not make the meat too dry. If you do, just add a little BBQ sauce till it holds together just well enough to form.

4. To form the burgers, I use about ½ to ¾ cup of the meat. I form it by making the ball and throwing it into each hand, compacting the meat down and together a few times. Then, I form it into a hamburger patty. If you get 93/7 meat, there is no need to put a hole in the middle. It will not shrink too much, just focus on making a patty that's 3 to 4 inches across.

5.     I like to cook on a pellet smoker, but any of the preferred choices will be fine to use. I shoot for a degree range of 375 – 425 degrees.  After the grill is preheated, cook burgers for three to four minutes on each side. Only flip once. For medium-rare, cook two to three minutes on higher heat for both sides and serve. Once the burger is cooked, place your favorite cheese on top, close lid, and let it melt for two to three minutes. Take off the heat and serve!  (For sides for this dish, check out the sides section in this book for ideas!).

☐

# Stuffed Jalapeno Popper Burgers

Ingredients:
- ☐ 3 pounds ground beef
- ☐ 1 to 1 ½ cups BBQ sauce – use your favorite brand
- ☐ 1 tablespoon minced garlic
- ☐ 2 eggs
- ☐ ¼ to ½ cup Italian breadcrumbs
- ☐ 1 large container of whipped cream cheese
- ☐ 1 cup of shredded fiesta cheese or shredded Colby and Monterey jack cheese
- ☐ 1 tablespoon of chile habanero hot sauce (Green salsa in Spanish food aisle) or any habanero salsa should work
- ☐ 2 packs of big Hawaiian hamburger buns

Preferred cooking: Gas, Charcoal, Pellet, or Smoker grill.
Preheat your grill to between 375 degrees and 425 degrees
Instructions:
1.     In a small mixing bowl, mix all the whipped cream cheese, shredded cheese, and habanero sauce. Mix thoroughly and set aside.
2.     In a separate large mixing bowl, mix the wet ingredients--BBQ sauce, minced garlic, and eggs with the beef and mix thoroughly.
3.     Mix in the Italian breadcrumbs until the meat holds together but does not crumble! If it becomes too dry, add BBQ sauce to get the correct consistency.

4.      To form the burgers, I use about ½ to ¾ cup of the meat. I form it by making the ball and throwing it into each hand, compacting the meat down and together a few times. Next, take your thumb and press a deep hole into your meatball mixture and make a wide opening. You then add a spoonful of the cream cheese mixture into that hole. Once the cream cheese mixture is inside, form the rest of the meat to cover the hole. The end result is the cream cheese mixture in the very center of your burger. Once formed into a ball-like shape, gently put on a baking sheet, and push down to form a patty. Do this with all the mixture.

5.      Preheat your grill to between 375 to 425 degrees. Once preheated, place the burgers on the grill and cook each side from five to seven on each side. Only flipping once. Less cooking time is needed for medium-rare, but I like to cook these burgers done with no pink inside since there is a mixture in the middle.

6.      After the burgers are fully cooked, place your favorite sliced cheese on top and close the lid for 2 to 3 minutes to let it melt. Once melted, remove from heat, and serve on large Hawaiian buns. (For sides for this dish, check out the sides section in this book for ideas!).

☐

# Bacon Jalapeno BBQ Cheeseburger Meatloaf

Ingredients:
- ☐ 4 to 5 pounds ground beef - 93/7 preferred
- ☐ 1 pound bacon any kind (thick-cut takes longer to crisp up so makes meatloaf more well done)
- ☐ 4 cups of shredded fiesta cheese or shredded Colby and Monterey jack cheese
- ☐ 3 eggs
- ☐ 1 ½ cups of Italian breadcrumbs
- ☐ Favorite BBQ sauce
- ☐ 1 tablespoon garlic powder
- ☐ 3 or 4 minced jalapenos
- ☐ 1 to 2 tablespoons oil or spray oil

Preferred cooking: Glass casserole dish or deep baking pan for cooking in the oven.
Preheat oven to 400 degrees.
Instructions:
1. Mix beef, BBQ sauce, eggs, and jalapenos and observe mixture.
2. Add in breadcrumbs slowly to make sure the mixture holds together but do not over crumb your meat mixture. If it becomes too dry, just add a little BBQ sauce to make it moister. You want a happy medium of dry and wet.
3. Oil the pan or dish (See preferred cooking instructions). You can use spray oil or regular oil. I use spray olive oil on most cooking surfaces.
4. Divide the meat in half. Put one half in the oiled pan or dish and spread it out in an even layer.
5. Take 4 cups or 4 big handfuls of shredded cheese and place on top of meat mixture you just spread in dish or pan.

6.      Take the other half of your meat mixture and flatten it on the counter or a cutting board. Place this sheet of meat on top of what's in the pan.

7.      Make a loaf by connecting the two sheets of meat. The result is a loaf with all the cheese in the center. You now have a loaf-like shape to your meatloaf.

8.      Place a bacon weave over the top of your meatloaf for best results. You can also just lay the bacon across in a layer and then another layer opposite of that. But I personally like to weave my bacon. A quick Internet search for "bacon weave" will give you a good idea of what to do.

9.      Place loaf into the oven and bake until the bacon on top of the loaf is crispy. You also can cook it to an internal temperature of 150 degrees.

10.     Once cooking is complete, remove from the oven. Serve after letting it rest for 5 to 10 minutes.

☐

# Amazing Meatballs

Ingredients:
- ☐ Olive oil spray
- ☐ 3 pounds ground beef- 93/7 preferred
- ☐ 1 ½ cups BBQ sauce – use your favorite brand
- ☐ 1 tablespoon garlic powder
- ☐ 1 tablespoon seasoned salt
- ☐ 1 tablespoon black pepper
- ☐ 2 eggs
- ☐ 1 cup Italian breadcrumbs
- ☐ 1 tablespoon Italian seasoning

Preferred cooking: Use flat baking sheet nonstick with oil spray or non-spray preheat oven to 425 degrees.

Instructions:

1. Mix ground beef, BBQ sauce, and eggs. Mix well.

2. Add dry ingredients. Mix in garlic powder, seasoned salt, black pepper, and Italian seasoning. Mix well.

3. Add breadcrumbs but do so slowly until the mixture is well put together but not too dry. If you make it too dry, just add a little BBQ sauce to find that even mix between wet and dry.

4. Once everything is mixed very well, start to form meatballs, I use a larger spoon almost 1 tablespoon to scoop and then form meatballs. Roll meat into balls. Try a few to make sure meatballs are well-formed and not falling apart. If consistency is right, roll all mixture into meatballs.

5. Spray baking pan covering the entire pan evenly. Place meatballs on the baking sheet and place the baking sheet in the oven.

6. I usually cook meatballs until I can smell them. This should take roughly 45 minutes to cook fully. To test, cut open one meatball to verify there is no pink inside—then they are ready to serve.

# Cheesy Meatball Subs

Ingredients:

Refer to the "Amazing Meatballs" recipe above and use the same meatballs for this recipe.

- ☐ Buns - Hoagie, Sub or French bread is preferred
- ☐ Minced garlic
- ☐ 2 teaspoons seasoned salt
- ☐ 2 sticks of butter or 1 cup of real salted butter
- ☐ Italian seasoning
- ☐ 1 tablespoon minced garlic
- ☐ Parmesan and Mozzarella
- ☐ Marinara sauce two 12- to 15-ounce jars (Spaghetti sauce will work also.)

Instructions:

Preferred cooking: 12- to 15-inch skillet that is 1 to 3 inches deep. Baking pan for toasting bread.

1. Make meatballs from my amazing meatball recipe. Once cooked, set aside.

2. Melt both sticks of butter in a small mixing bowl. Add minced garlic, Italian seasoning, and seasoned salt. Mix well then set aside.

3. Place cooked meatballs in a 12- to 15-inch skillet that is 1 to 3 inches deep. Pour both jars of marinara sauce into the pan with meatballs. Place lid on top and cook at medium heat stirring every 3 to 5 minutes until sauce and meatballs are heated.

4. While that is cooking, cut open your hoagie buns or bread of your choice. Place on the baking sheet with the insides facing up.

5. Use a basting brush to coat the bread with the butter mixture. Coat bread evenly with the mixture. Once evenly spread on bread, add a small amount of parmesan and mozzarella cheese. Use enough to sprinkle it on the bread over the butter mixture, but do not put a ton of cheese on.

6.     Set oven to high broil and place bread into the oven. Check bread every minute or so. Be careful not to let it burn. You may need to turn the pan to toast bread evenly. Once well toasted but not burnt remove from oven and place on the counter for serving.

7.     Remove meatballs and sauce from heat when heated through.

8.     Add 3 to 4 meatballs and sauce to hoagie or sub. Sprinkle mozzarella cheese over the top and serve.

Grape Jelly Meat Balls

Ingredients:

Refer to the "Amazing Meatballs" recipe above and use the same meatballs for this recipe.

☐     2 large jars of grape jelly 12- to 15-ounce jars

☐     4 jars of chili sauce (Heinz or any brand), 6- to 8-ounce jars


Preferred cooking:  Crockpot with low to medium-high setting.

Instructions:

1.     Make meatballs from my amazing meatball recipe. Once cooked, set aside.

2.     Turn crockpot on medium heat.

3.     Place cooked meatballs in the crockpot. Pour all grape jelly and chili sauce over meatballs. Place a lid on top of the crockpot and cook until heated well. I usually cook until the mixture is boiling a little, then it's ready to serve!

4.     Serve by itself for tailgating or just for any sporting event that needs an appetizer.

☐

# Spaghetti with Meatballs

Ingredients:

Refer to the "Amazing Meatballs" recipe above and use the same meatballs for this recipe.

- ☐ 2 to 3 pounds of angel hair or thin spaghetti noodles
- ☐ 2 cups of olive oil (optional)
- ☐ 2 to 3 teaspoons sea salt
- ☐ 1 to 2 tablespoons Italian seasoning to taste

Sauce:

- ☐ 2 10- to 12-ounce cans tomato sauce
- ☐ 2 tablespoons Italian seasoning
- ☐ 2 tablespoons minced garlic
- ☐ 1 large sweet onion or yellow onion
- ☐ Salt and pepper to taste

Preferred cooking: Tall pot for boiling noodles, large strainer, 12- to 15-inch skillet 1 to 3 inches deep

Instructions:

1. Make meatballs from my amazing meatball recipe. Once cooked, set aside.

2. Once meatballs are cooked, place in skillet and add all sauce ingredients. Mix well and let simmer with the lid on top.

3. While sauce is simmering on low, fill deep pot ¾ full of 4 to 6 quarts of water and boil. Add sea salt and 1 cup of olive oil. Boil noodles till they are kind of firm but not so soft they mush together. Check noodles every few minutes by tasting one noodle at a time checking texture and firmness. When noodles are cooked and perfect, use a strainer to drain into the sink. Only strain for less than 10 seconds and put back in the pot. You can add any oil, but I add 1 cup of olive oil into noodles or more and add a couple of tablespoons of Italian seasoning to the noodles, but you can serve them without out or Italian seasoning if you'd like.

4.     Your spaghetti sauce should be finished simmering, so remove both noodles and sauce from heat and serve!

# Korean Beef Bowl

Ingredients:

- ☐  4 cups rice
- ☐  3 pounds ground beef - 93/7 preferred
- ☐  3 tablespoons sesame oil
- ☐  3 tablespoons minced garlic
- ☐  1 ½ teaspoons minced ginger
- ☐  1 ½ cups brown sugar
- ☐  1 ½ cups soy sauce (low sodium optional)
- ☐  3 teaspoons crushed red pepper (for spice)
- ☐  Salt and pepper to taste
- ☐  Chives (2 stalks)
- ☐  Sushi seasoning
- ☐  Sesame seeds
- ☐  4 jalapenos (for added spice)

Preferred Cooking:  Cook in a large skillet for browning meet one to two inches deep, if possible.

Instructions:

1.      Cook the rice first.  Add 3 cups of water to a medium-size pot and boil. Once water is boiling, stir 4 cups of rice into boiling water. Mix together, then wait for it to boil again. Stir and cover while placing on low heat. Simmer covered for 15 to 20 minutes. DO NOT UN-COVER until the time has elapsed.  You are looking for rice that is sticky or just doesn't have any water left in pan at the end of the 20 minutes. If the rice still has water in it, cover and cook until water is gone—but do not burn!

2.      While rice is cooking, add the beef to the skillet and start to brown meat. I like to add in jalapenos and extra sesame seeds into meat mixture when halfway browned.  When the meat is done, add minced garlic, sesame oil, soy sauce, crushed red pepper. Mix well with the meat.

3.      Once the mixture starts to boil a little, add brown sugar. Stir and mix well until dissolved.

4.      Add in minced ginger and mix well.

5.      Let simmer for 5 minutes or until you have a good consistency. You do not want your mixture to be watery. You want a nice glazed texture.

6.      Remove from heat. I like to add salt and pepper at this point for taste and extra flavor but isn't always needed. Once the rice is complete, remove from heat, also.

7.      Before serving, chop up chives and have sesame seeds and sushi seasoning on the counter next to your completed dish.

8.      Now it is time to serve! Spoon rice into a bowl and add meat mixture over rice, sprinkle chives and sesame seeds, and sushi seasoning all over the top. Enjoy!

☐

# Chicken Dishes:

# Chicken Adobo with rice

Ingredients:
- ☐ 5 pounds chicken thighs – bone-in with skin
- ☐ 5 pounds chicken legs – bone-in with skin
- ☐ 5 cups soy sauce - low sodium
- ☐ 5 cups white vinegar
- ☐ 5 cups water
- ☐ 5 bay leaves
- ☐ 5 teaspoons ground pepper
- ☐ 3 tablespoons minced garlic
- ☐ 1 large can adobo chilis or 2 small cans
- ☐ 4 cups Basmati or Jasmine rice

Preferred cooking: Cook in a large deep pot. Caution: This is a spicy dish, but you can choose not to use chilis if you do not like spice.

Instructions:

1.  Add soy sauce, white vinegar, water, bay leaves, ground pepper, minced garlic, and adobo chilis in a pot together and stir well.

Place on medium-high heat until the mixture starts to boil, then add all the chicken. You want all the chicken to be covered in the mixture. So, if needed, add a little more water until the sauce is just over chicken. Cover with a lid and reduce heat down to medium-low, so the mixture remains at a slow boil.

2.  While that is cooking, add 3 cups of water to a medium-size pan and boil. Once boiling, add rice. When it starts to boil again, stir it well, put a lid on it, and turn the heat down to low or simmer. Cook for 15 to 20 minutes. Do not look at or check rice until the 15 to 20-minute mark. You want your rice to be somewhat sticky with no water left in the pan. Once completed, remove from heat. A rice cooker helps if you have one. Just always add ¾ cup water to 1 cup rice for good results.

3.     Once the rice is cooked, your chicken adobo should be completed as well! Cut into the chicken to ensure that it is cooked all the way through. If cooked through, remove everything from heat. Serve one chicken thigh and one leg on top of a bowl full of rice. Add juices, if desired, serve and enjoy!

# Creamy Rotisserie Chicken with Rice

Ingredients:
- ☐ 4 cups Jasmine rice
- ☐ 2 rotisserie chickens pre-cooked from the store (or 4 chicken breasts baked at 400 for 45 minutes until done in the middle)
- ☐ 2 cans of cream of chicken soup
- ☐ 4 cans of cream of mushroom soup
- ☐ Salt and pepper to taste
- ☐ 3 to 5 cups shredded fiesta-style cheese or Colby and Monterey jack

Preferred cooking: Cook in a deep large casserole glass dish or deep pan. Preheat to 350 to 375 degrees.

1. Cook 4 cups of rice by adding 3 cups of water into a medium size pan and bring to a boil. Once the water is boiling, add rice and stir. Bring to a boil again, stir, and place lid on top. Turn heat down to low or simmer. Once the rice is cooked, oil or butter a glass dish. Place all the rice into a mixing bowl.
2. Next, add all ingredients, remove all the meat from the rotisserie chicken and chop up or chop up 4 cups cooked chicken breasts into small pieces.
3. Add the chicken to the large mixing bowl with the rice. Then, add all cream of chicken soups and cream of mushroom soups and salt and pepper to taste. Once all contents are equally mixed, add to a large casserole dish or deep baking pan.
4. Add cheese on top—a nice thick layer over the top—and put in the oven. Cook until the cheese is fully melted and crispy on top!
5. Once cooked, remove from oven let sit for 10 minutes before serving!

☐

# Chicken and Beef Fajitas

Ingredients:

- ☐     5 to 7 pounds of chicken thighs - boneless and skinless
- ☐     4 packages or 2 to 3 pounds of flank steak
- ☐     4 12-ounce bottles of any garlic and herb marinade
- ☐     2 packages of small tortillas (20 in each pack – minimum)
- ☐     1 large container of sour cream
- ☐     1 bag of any shredded cheese for tacos or fajitas
- ☐     2 large sweet onions or yellow onions
- ☐     2 large green peppers of 3 small
- ☐     2 tablespoons minced garlic
- ☐     1 stick salted real butter
- ☐     3 teaspoon seasoned salt

Preferred cooking: I like to grill meat on grill gas, charcoal, pellet, or smoker grill. Marinate meat for a minimum of 2 hours, I like to marinate all day until I'm ready to cook.

Instructions:

1. Marinate chicken and beef in separate bowls using two bottles of marinade for each bowl. Stir, cover, and set in the fridge to marinate for at least 2 hours.

2. When the meat is marinated and ready to cook, preheat the grill or preferred cooking above to between 375 and 425 degrees. Prepare the peppers by getting a large piece of tin foil and chopping up all onion and green peppers and place on tin foil.

3.    Chop up the butter into a few small pieces or pats and place on top of peppers with seasoned salt and minced garlic. Mix together with hands and wrap up the contents tightly in the foil. If need be, make your own pouch then add another piece of foil to wrap it tighter.

4.    When the grill is preheated, add the chicken to the grill first. When chicken is almost cooked through, add the pepper pouch to the grill.

5.    When the chicken is fully cooked (20 minutes or more), remove from the grill. Add the beef. Keep a close eye on the flank steak, and make sure not to let it burn.

6.    By this time, the chicken and beef are done, the peppers should be done. Check and make sure the peppers are easy to tear apart and limp and onions are transparent.

7.    When everything is done, remove everything from heat. Take the meat to the kitchen and chop meat into bite-size pieces.

8.    Serve in separate bowls and serve peppers in another separate bowl. Place cheese, sour cream, hot

sauces, and tortillas on the counter (heating tortillas is optional).  Then, dinner is served!

☐

# Chicken and/or Beef Taco Salad

Ingredients:
- ☐ 3 to 4 pounds of boneless chicken thighs and/or beef
- ☐ 2 large sweet onions or yellow onions
- ☐ 3 or 4 Roma tomatoes
- ☐ 1 each red leaf, iceberg, and romaine lettuce
- ☐ Doritos
- ☐ 2 diced jalapenos
- ☐ Shredded fiesta cheese or Colby and Monterey Jack shredded cheese
- ☐ 1 large container sour cream
- ☐ Any hot sauces
- ☐ Cilantro
- ☐ Taco seasoning:
  - o 3 tablespoons chili powder
  - o 3 teaspoons garlic powder
  - o 3 teaspoons onion powder
  - o 2 teaspoons crushed red pepper flakes
  - o 2 teaspoons dried oregano
  - o 2 teaspoons paprika
  - o 2 teaspoons cumin
  - o 2 teaspoons black pepper
  - o 2 teaspoons seasoned salt
  - o 2 teaspoons cayenne
- ☐ 3 to 5 cups water

Preferred cooking: If you cook both types of meat, make sure you add the exact amounts for both meats. The measurements are shown for one meat. If you do both chicken and beef, just add the same ingredients and measurements for both meats.

Instructions:
1. Brown the ground beef and/or chicken thighs.

2.    Add diced jalapenos and one onion to each if you cook both beef and chicken. Cook until meat is fully cooked.  Add all the taco seasonings and mix well.

3.    Add water until meat and seasoning mixture is wet but not soaking. Add 3 cups and mix well. See if you need to add more for each beef and or chicken.  Once that is complete, put a lid over the meat and reduce heat to low or simmer.

4.    While that's simmering, wash and cut up the salad. I like to break it up with my hands and rinse it as I break it up. Throw away all brown pieces or hard, inedible pieces. I also break up all three heads of salad, but you can choose how much you want to serve.  Once cleaned and broken up in a strainer, pat dry and place salad in a large bowl for serving.

5.    By this time, your meat and seasoning mixture(s) should be done. Remove from heat.

6.    Serve the taco salad in a line. Salad first, then meat, then cheese, Doritos, sour cream and hot sauces, Roma tomatoes, and finally diced onion diced. All items are served in separate bowls.

# Loddy Doddy Everybody:

These dishes include a few recipes that we used to do multi-station dinners so you can cook for ten people, or you can cook for half that if you choose. (These dishes do include pork).

# Dr. Prepper Pulled Pork

Ingredients:

☐ 8 to 12 pounds pork butt-bone In (I would say: 1 feeds 6 to 8 decent-sized guys eating two portions. If you're serving more people than that, buy another one the same size.)

☐ 1 large bottle of your favorite BBQ sauce (24 to 32 ounces of sauce)

☐ Pork rub

Seasoned salt, Greek poultry seasoning, black pepper, garlic powder, onion powder, cayenne for some spice. For my rub, I use 4 tablespoons of all of this and add it to a shaker. For cayenne and black pepper, use only 1 ½ to 2 tablespoons. Or, you can buy your own specific rub. I like to travel and buy new rubs to BBQ with, so I encourage yawl to do the same!

☐ Dr. Prepper or any soda dark in a 2—one soda for each pork butt you decide to cook

☐ Optional: Aluminum Roasting pan 1 for each pork butt. Get a medium-sized pan, just big enough for the pork butt to fit in.

☐ Heavy-duty foil

☐ 2 packages Hawaiian Bun sliders (24 packs)

(Also see my Slaw Texas Style in the SIDES section. It is the perfect side to go with this pulled pork).

Preferred Cooking: I prefer to cook on a charcoal, gas, or pellet smoker grill, but I will add instructions for oven also.

Instructions:

1. Cover your pork butt(s) fully on all sides and crevices in the rub of your choice or use the rub in the ingredients I posted above.

2.      Once covered with rub, preheat your grill (or skillet if a grill is not available). For the grill, I crank it up to 450 degrees. If you use a skillet, put some oil olive oil or vegetable oil in the bottom of the skillet--1 or 2 cups will work. Once skillet and grill are heated, sear all sides of pork butt for about 2 to 3 minutes on each side until it has a golden-brown look to that particular side.  Sear all sides, top, bottom, and edges—all of it!

3.      Oven: Once seared, you preheat oven to 250 degrees

Grill:  Once seared, set your grill to the temp of around 250 degrees—give or take a few degrees for the swinging temps. If it drops too low, crank it up to 275 degrees.

4.      While you are pre-heating, get a 2- to 3-inch deep baking pan (or the disposable pans I mentioned in the ingredients section) and place each pork butt into their own pan.

5.      Pour dark soda over the top and then wrap the whole pan tightly in heavy-duty tin foil to completely cover the top no leaks or holes present.

6.      Cooking should take 6 to 8 hours. The longer, the better. When it gets to the 8-hour mark, check frequently. You can turn it up to 300 degrees if it isn't cooking too fast.  Be patient and cook till it falls apart! Cook to a minimum of 160 degrees internal temperature, but it's okay to cook higher. Most meats I smoke, I keep smoking until its 190 degrees just for the extra added meat that falls apart.

7.      Once completed, serve on Hawaiian bun sliders. (Also see my Slaw Texas Style in the SIDES section. It is the perfect side to go with this pulled pork).

☐

# Pinto Bean Soup

Ingredients:

This recipe is going to be a little different. We used this recipe when we invite everyone to dinner, and it was station fridge cleanout day. What I list in this section will be some of the stuff that we had in our fridges that we used instead of throwing away.

☐ 3 pounds pinto beans or three16-ounce bags

☐ Vegetables: onions, red, orange, or green peppers, jalapenos, potatoes, garlic, squash, tomatoes, green chilis, etc.

☐ Meat: turkey necks, ham hocks, ham bones, sausage of any kind of meat—deer, elk, pork, Cajun, beef chunks. Shoot for 4 to 5 pounds of meat.

☐ Seasoning:

o Season salt

o Black pepper

☐ Chicken and beef broth

☐ Water

Preferred Cooking & Prep: I like to cook this meal and a big stockpot. You can use any pot. Just make sure it's big enough to fit everything in it. Soak beans the night before in plenty of water for at least 8 hours. I like to add a tiny bit of salt and stir them a few times before bed. When you wake up in the morning before you start cooking, remove the bean husks and bad beans—those that don't look like the other ones just to cook your soup clear of all the stuff you don't need in it. Some beans may need help getting their husks off. Stir them and help the ones that are coming off. It doesn't need to be perfect; you just want to remove most of the bean husks, especially the loose ones.

Instructions:

1.　　After cleaning your bean pot, start by taking everything out of the fridge that you are going to throw away. Be sure that it is still okay to cook. Put the veggies on one side and the meats on another.

The list of veggies and meats I have above are great things to add. So, whatever is missing with the veggies, grab a few more things that you do not have. With the meats, if you don't have any meat, go to the store and grab a few things. I always add ham hocks and sausage for this. But, if you have leftover meat items, you can add them to this dish!

2.　　After you have everything separated and have been to the store, start by getting a large skillet. Cut up all veggies into diced pieces and add them to the pan. Add garlic seasoned salt and pepper to taste. Add oil to help start cooking and put the heat on medium-high. Cook the veggies well done. There is no limit to how many veggies you use, so don't be shy!

While cooking veggies, add water ¾ the way up the pan of beans and start to boil the beans. Add veggies to the beans and stir well.

3.　　Finally, take the meats that you have and do exactly what you did with the veggies. Dice it all up and sear the meat. Once the meat is seared, add to the pot. If you have ham hocks or ham bones, just throw those in automatically.　　Stir contents well, and let it come to a boil. Turn the heat down to medium and let the soup boil at that temp for 2 hours covered with a lid or foil. Make sure it's a slower boil and not a rolling boil. After slow boiling for 2 hours, reduce to a low simmer and keep the lid on for another 2 to 3 hours.

4.　　The soup should be ready to serve! Serve with bread or cornbread. Great meal for the winter!

☐

# Green Chili Sloppers

Ingredients:
- [ ] 1 10- to 12-pound pork butt
- [ ] 3 large sweet onions
- [ ] 1 large white onion
- [ ] 7 cloves garlic or 3 tablespoons minced garlic
- [ ] 4 32-ounce cartons chicken broth
- [ ] 4 28-ounce cans fire-roasted diced tomatoes
- [ ] 3 pounds potatoes (optional)
- [ ] 4 cups green chilis-hot or mild, roasted, and shell peeled off

(Every year I find someone who sells green chilis and have them roast them for me. Then, I take them home and shell them and freeze them in quart-size bags. This is a great way to keep green chilis for a while. They are great for an easy green chili set up).

- [ ] Seasoned salt, Greek poultry seasoning, black pepper, garlic powder, onion powder, cayenne for some spice. For my rub, I do 4 tablespoons of all of this and add it to a shaker. For cayenne and black pepper, use only 1 ½ to 2 tablespoons. Or, you can buy your own specific rub. I like to travel and buy new rubs to BBQ with, so I encourage yawl to do the same!
- [ ] Sour cream
- [ ] Shredded cheese fiesta blend
- [ ] Burgers:
- [ ] 1 egg
- [ ] 2 cups favorite BBQ sauce
- [ ] Salt and pepper 2 TSP each
- [ ] ¼ cup Italian breadcrumbs.
- [ ] 4 LBS Ground Beef 93/7
- [ ] Favorite sliced cheese for each burger
- [ ] Hawaiian Buns Large!

Preferred Cooking:  For green chili, use a big stockpot. For burgers, I prefer to use a grill—gas, charcoal, or pellet smoker.

Instructions:

1.      Make the green chili. Start by seasoning your pork butt with the rub I have in the ingredients section on all sides. Sear on a grill at 425 degrees or in a skillet with oil on medium-high. Sear all sides and crevasses. Once golden brown on all sides set aside.

2.      Add green chilis, 3 diced sweet onions, minced garlic, all chicken broth, all fire-roasted tomatoes, and all 4 cups of green chilis and stir well. Place burner on high and boil contents stirring every 2 to 3 minutes.

3.      Once boiling, add seared pork butt into the mix. Make sure you have a big enough pot so it doesn't overflow! Cover with lid and turn the heat down to low or simmer. Let it cook for 3 to 4 hours or until meat is falling apart!

4.      If you choose to use potatoes to thicken it up, add 3 pounds of potatoes during the last 40 minutes or so of cooking or when you notice meat starting to fall apart. Make sure you dice potatoes into ½-inch by ½-inch pieces before adding. Clean the outside of potatoes well with a sponge or brush.  Now your green chili is close to being done.

5.      Preheat your grill to 425 degrees. Mix your hamburger, egg, seasonings salt and pepper, Italian breadcrumbs, and favorite BBQ sauce. Your mixture should not be too wet but firm. If not, add BBQ Sauce for wetness or breadcrumbs slowly to dry it out a little.  Once you have a good mix, form your burger patties well. Once all are formed, throw them onto the grill.

6.      Cook both sides for 3 to 4 minutes each. Only flipping once! Once cooked thoroughly, remove from grill. Now you are almost ready!

7.     Dice up one white onion and put it in a bowl as a side. Set out your sour cream and shredded cheese. I serve this dish by taking a burger and putting it into a bun both top and bottom and placing it into a bowl. Then, pour green chili all over it--smothering it up to the top of the bowl. Next, garnish with shredded cheese, sour cream, and fresh chopped white onion and serve!
This dish is my most favorite dish to make for friends. It's a local dish where I'm from (Pueblo, Colorado). They have a competition between cooks every year to see whose Green Chili Sloppers are the best!
☐

# Epic Sides:

These sides can go with almost any dish in this book. These are mostly my own creations I'm excited for you to add them to any meal. They make our meal not just good—but great!

# Slaw Texas Style

Ingredients:
- ☐ 1 head of cabbage
- ☐ 1 jar of mayo (the good stuff not cheap)
- ☐ ½ pound carrots
- ☐ Seasonings are estimated - I do it for my own taste. I advise you to do the same.
- o 2 teaspoons cayenne
- o 2 teaspoons black pepper
- ☐ 2 tablespoons white vinegar
- ☐ 3 to 4 tablespoons of your local fresh honey

Preferred Cooking: Use a giant mixing bowl.

Instructions:

1. Remove the core from the bottom of the cabbage by making a V. Cut into it at an angle just to cut out the core on both sides and save as much of the cabbage as possible. After this, dice up the cabbage into 1-inch by 1-inch pieces and shred into a bowl.

2. Add a full jar of mayo and mix well.

3. Chop up carrots super small—do the best you can. I cut the slices down the carrot ¼-inch thick then cut those pieces in half. Or fourths if the pieces are large. Once carrots are chopped and diced into small pieces, mix into the cabbage mix.

4. Add the white vinegar and black pepper.

5. Add the honey, then the cayenne pepper to taste. I mix well as I slowly add those two ingredients. Stop adding when you have a sweet but spicy flavor. It should not be too overwhelming from either the honey or cayenne pepper. You should have a nice, but not overpowering vinegar flavor also. If not, you can always add a touch more white vinegar.

6. Now that the coleslaw is done, you can enjoy it with pulled pork or just a side whenever you BBQ or grill out!

# Smooth Poblano Salsa

Ingredients:

- ☐　6 Large Hass or regular avocadoes
- ☐　3 Large sweet onions
- ☐　2 Large poblano peppers
- ☐　4 jalapenos
- ☐　2 to 3 tablespoons minced garlic
- ☐　2 bundles of cilantro
- ☐　3 teaspoons seasoned salt
- ☐　4 Limes
- ☐　5 Roma tomatoes
- ☐　Cracked pepper to taste
- ☐　½ tablespoon olive oil (optional)

Preferred Cooking: Use the biggest blender or food processor you have.

Instructions:

1.　Peel the avocadoes. The best way is to research and watch a video on how to cut first before removing contents. You slice down the middle of the avocadoes and all the way around till it splits in half. Take your knife in one hand while holding the side with the pit in it in your other hand, making sure your hand is clear of the fruit side of the pitted side and chop hard at the seed. It should get stuck in the seed. Twist the seed out of the avocado, do this to all of them before chopping. Once all seeds have been removed, make a grid-like pattern slicing down the avocado then across, making sure not to cut too deep and cutting yourself. Once you cut the grid, squeeze the avocado together. All the little squares should come out, do this to all the avocadoes and place contents in a blender.

2.      Take a medium-sized pot. Fill it ¾ the way up and turn on high to boil.  Once boiling, remove the shell of the onions, chop in half, and toss in the boiling water along with all the Roma tomatoes. You want to boil these until the tomatoes' skin is almost peeled off. When you lift them out of the water, they squish a little bit but do not fall apart—and the same with onions.

3.      While those are boiling, get a baking pan and coat your jalapenos and poblano peppers by hand with olive oil or any oil you have on hand.  Place them on the baking sheet and turn your oven to broil and put them in. Check them frequently. You want them to blister on all sides but not burn. The result will be a roasted pepper that is limp, not hard.

4.      By this time, your peppers onions and tomatoes are done!  Add onions and tomatoes to the blender and blend well.

5.      Cut off the stems of the jalapenos and poblano peppers (preferable leaving seeds in for spice, but you can take them out to make less spicy) and add them to the blender and blend well, adding 1 or 2 cups of the onion-tomato water you used to boil and blend well.

6.      Chop up the cilantro. Chop the ends off the 2 bundles—the ends that do not have leaves, roughly 1 inch off the bottom of the cilantro. Throw the leafy sides into the blender and blend well.

7.      Add garlic, cracked pepper, olive oil, and the juice of all 4 limes and blend well.

8.      Add salt at the very end for taste. I use chips to taste test.

Now you have an awesome salsa that will go with any dish or just as a side with chips! (This is my favorite salsa to use for fish and shrimp tacos)!

☐

# Home Fries!

Ingredients:
- ☐      4 large russet potatoes
- ☐      2 to 3 tablespoons bacon grease or olive oil
- ☐      3 teaspoons seasoned salt
- ☐      2 to 3 teaspoons cracked pepper

Preferred Cooking:  Large skillet with a lid.

Instructions:

1. Wash your potatoes very well, scrubbing the dirt off the outside of the potatoes.  Dice into small ¼- to ½-inch pieces. The sizing does not have to be perfect. Just make sure they are diced up pretty small.

2. Heat the pan to medium-high. Add bacon grease or olive oil. Stir well, so all potatoes are coated with the oil.  If you run out of grease or oil while cooking, just add a little more if necessary. Add salt and pepper towards the end of cooking for a little more to taste. Cook potatoes until they are nice and crispy on all sides and remove from heat. I like to let them settle on a paper towel to drain any excess grease before eating.

3. Serve and eat as a side for any meal!

☐

# Spanish Rice

Ingredients:
- ☐ 2 tablespoons olive oil
- ☐ 4 cups Jasmine or Basmati rice
- ☐ 2 12-ounce cans of Rotel
- ☐ 3 teaspoons seasoned salt
- ☐ 3 teaspoons black pepper

Preferred Cooking: Large skillet - 2 to 3 inches deep
Instructions:
1.    Place 4 cups rice into a deep skillet and mix in olive oil evenly to coat most of the rice. Turn the burner on high and use a wooden spoon and stir often until rice is browned.
2.    Once the rice is browned, leave on high and slowly add 3 cups of water. Be careful not to get steam burns!
3.    After all water is added, add Rotel. Mix well and add salt and pepper.
4.    Stir and mix well until the rice starts to boil again. Reduce heat to simmer or low and cover.
5.    Rice will be done when all water is gone. Do not remove the lid. This should take 20 minutes or so—check after 20 minutes as the rice should be cooked! Serve and enjoy!
☐

# Sweet Potato Fries

Ingredients:
- ☐ 4 Large sweet potatoes
- ☐ 3 teaspoons ground cinnamon
- ☐ Olive oil or coconut oil
- ☐ Seasoned salt

Preferred Cooking:  Baking sheet nonstick
Instructions:
1. Cut sweet potatoes up into ¼-inch thin fries.
2. Use olive or coconut oil and your hands to coat the sweet potato fries thoroughly!
3. Preheat oven to 425 degrees. Season fries lightly with seasoned salt.
4. Stick in the oven and cook them until a little darker than golden brown on all sides. Season lightly when you turn them every 8 minutes or so.
5. When done, pull them out of the oven and let them cool. While cooling, sprinkle ground cinnamon (optional) on top of sweet potato fries and serve!
- ☐

# The World's Best Garlic Bread

Ingredients:
Your favorite Hot dog buns this makes one large pan of garlic bread

- ☐ 2 sticks butter
- ☐ 1 ½ tablespoon minced garlic
- ☐ ½ tablespoon Italian seasoning
- ☐ Shaker parmesan cheese
- ☐ Shredded mozzarella cheese

Preferred Cooking:  Nonstick baking pan

Instructions:

1. Split apart hot dog buns and lay them inside up on the baking pan.
2. In a small mixing bowl, melt butter for 1:30 in the microwave then add in minced garlic and Italian seasoning and mix well.
3. Use a basting brush and brush the buttery contents all over the buns making sure to get an even coat. You don't have to use all of it but get a good amount of the garlic and seasoning on the bread—more than butter, if possible.
4. Shake a nice layer of parmesan over the buns. Use enough to do a nice coat, but not too thick. Do the same with the mozzarella.
5. Turn your oven on high broil and place your baking sheet in the oven. Stand next to it and keep a close eye on it. Make sure it does not burn.  You may have to turn the pan with a hot pad to make the whole pan brown evenly.
6. When the bread is golden brown, and the cheese is melted, remove from oven, and serve with your greatest pasta dishes or spaghetti! Or check out the meatball sub recipe. I used this recipe in addition to it. Enjoy!

☐

# Homemade Breakfasts:

# Homemade Jalapeno Biscuits and Gravy

Ingredients:

Biscuits:

- ☐ 4 cups all-purpose flour
- ☐ 2 tablespoons baking powder
- ☐ 2 ½ teaspoons seasoned salt
- ☐ 3 minced jalapenos (Do not add if you do not want them spicy.)
- ☐ 2 sticks butter or 8 ounces butter
- ☐ 1 ½ cups whole milk
- ☐

Gravy:

- ☐ 2 pounds or 2 rolls of sausage - 1 hot and 1 regular
- ☐ 1 pound thick-cut bacon
- ☐ 1 gallon whole milk
- ☐ ½ to ¾ cup all-purpose flour
- ☐ 3 to 4 minced jalapenos (optional for spice)
- ☐ Seasoned salt and cracked pepper for taste

Preferred Cooking: Biscuits on a large nonstick baking sheet. Gravy in a large deep pot.

Instructions:

1. Start by crisping up the thick-cut bacon. Once strips are nice and crispy, remove and place on paper towels to drain—hide so nobody steals your bacon!
2. Start your biscuits by adding flour, baking powder, minced jalapenos, (if using), and salt. Mix well.
3. Melt butter in the microwave and pour into flour mixture mixing well with a metal spoon. You will have to mix these contents for a little while until thick. Make sure there are no lumps.
4. Preheat oven to 400 degrees. Oil baking pan lightly.

5.    Scoop biscuit mixture with the mixing spoon and drop onto the pan. Thus, they are called "drop biscuits." Use approximately ¼ to ½ cup for each biscuit.

6.    Once all are dropped onto the pan, put in the oven and bake for 20 minutes or until they rise and are golden brown on top.

7.    While biscuits are cooking, start browning the sausage in a medium-size deep pan. When almost all sausage is brown, add jalapenos during the last 3 to 4 minutes of browning.

8.    When the meat is completely brown, add flour mixture until all the grease is gone. Stir flour well into the meat. I use ½ cup of flour, but if you need to, sprinkle in a little more.

9.    Once the grease is soaked up, slowly add a gallon of milk. Add a little at a time. Pour with one hand while stirring with the other. Pour and stir until the milk is mixed in well. It will start out thick and get thinner as you mix in the milk. Add milk slowly because if you add it too fast, you can make it to watery. I usually add a little more than half a gallon—when the gravy stops getting thick and remains at a constant consistency. One way to tell if your gravy is almost done is to use a scoop spoon without slits. Scoop a spoonful and pour it out. If it sticks to the spoon with a nice coat after pouring out, you have a good consistency. Do not let your gravy boil. Stir constantly making sure it doesn't burn on the bottom. Turn down heat if need be!

10.    Add seasoned salt and pepper for flavor. Add seasoning a little at a time and have a friend help taste by using multiple small spoons.

11.    Once it is good, crunch up the crispy, thick-cut bacon and add it all into the gravy!

12.    Remove gravy from heat, and it is ready to serve.

13.    Once biscuits are golden brown, remove them from the oven. I normally make someone watch them for me while I make the gravy.

14.    Now you are ready to eat a meal of homemade biscuits and gravy! Serve by placing biscuits on a plate and smother with gravy!!

☐

# Eggs Be Gone Scramble

Ingredients:
- ☐ 18 pack of eggs (I have my own chickens. I use them and it makes this dish better!)
- ☐ 1 pound thick-cut bacon
- ☐ 3 large russet potatoes
- ☐ shredded cheese

Optional:
- ☐ Tortillas

Preferred Cooking:  Use a large 10- to 12-inch skillet that is 2 to 3 inches deep

Instructions:

This recipe is super simple. I always made this for a quick breakfast for the guys at the station in the morning.

1. Clean the potatoes thoroughly and dice them up small.
2. You can cook the bacon separately, but I just chop the bacon up into 1-inch square pieces and cook it with taters.
3. Once bacon and taters are crispy on all sides, crack all 18 eggs or farm fresh eggs into a bowl and scramble.
4. Once scrambled, add them to the mixture stirring occasionally as the eggs cook.
5. Once eggs are almost fully cooking, or the wetness is gone, add a nice thick layer of shredded cheese. Cover with a lid and remove from heat.
6. Wait a couple of minutes until the cheese fully melts, and it is ready to serve! Serve with my homemade salsa recipe in sides!

☐

# In Closing:

I had an amazing time making this book: The Cookbook & Guide for Your Probie Firefighters & First Responders and an even greater time creating lifelong family and friends in the brotherhood and sisterhood of first responders through cooking and in my career.

I hope this book motivates you to follow whatever passion you have! Wherever this book finds you in life, I hope it finds you well. I hope it motivates you to do what you have always wanted to do or have dreamed of doing. This book alone has pushed me outside my comfort level to create a business not only about cooking and the fire department but it has motivated me to create a business that helps people in every aspect of their life—whether it be helping people build businesses or just wanting to build relationships and teaching others about the fire service and my passion of cooking.

Fire and Entrepreneurship Services is a company that I am creating not only to help people and their way of thinking and living but also to help people in need in their everyday lives. Thank you for joining me on this journey, and please stay tuned and follow for more content.

Good luck and God bless to all my friends, family, future friends, and a special thanks to my brothers and sisters in arms and first responders I have worked with or will work with in the future.

Thank you all for your sacrifice and daily selfless service. "First in last out!"

☐

For more content, please follow me at:
My YouTube page: @ Fire and Entrepreneurship
Services.
My website:
https://wordpress.com/view/fire-and-
entrepreneurship-services.com
My Email:
fireentrepreneurshipservices@gmail.com
If you liked this book Please Wright a Review@:
https://www.amazon.com/dp/B08GL6GPCW#cu
stomerReviews

Printed in Great Britain
by Amazon

51783183R00046